Knowing God

"God, I want to know You better!"

By Jane L. Fryar
Edited by Thomas J. Doyle

Editorial assistant: Marilyn T. Weber

Unless otherwise stated, Scripture taken from THE HOLY BIBLE: NEW INTERNATIONAL VERSION®. Copyright © 1973, 1978, 1984 by International Bible Society. Used by permission of Zondervan Bible Publishers. All rights reserved.

The "NIV" and "New International Version" trademarks are registered in the United States Patent and Trademark Office by International Bible Society. Use of either trademark requires the permission of International Bible Society.

Scripture quotations marked NKJV are from the New King James edition, copyright © 1979, 1980, 1982. Used by permission.

Verses marked TLB are taken from THE LIVING BIBLE, © 1971 by Tyndale House Publishers, Wheaton, IL. Used by permission.

Copyright © 1993 Concordia Publishing House
3558 South Jefferson Avenue, St. Louis, MO 63118-3968
Manufactured in the United States of America.

All rights reserved. No part of this publication may be reproduced, stored in a retrieval system, or transmitted, in any form or by any means, electronic, mechanical, photocopying, recording, or otherwise, without the prior written permission of Concordia Publishing House.

2 3 4 5 6 7 8 9 10   02 01 00 99 98 97 96 95

By mutual agreement . . .
and in the Holy Spirit's power

We will attend each session unless an
    emergency prevents our attendance.
We will listen to each other and show one another
    Christ-like love and concern.
We will contribute to the discussion in positive ways
    as we are able to do that.
We will rely on the Holy Scriptures as our final authority,
    knowing that human ideas and opinions,
    even the ideas and opinions of God's people,
    will likely stray from God's truth from time to time.
We will keep everything we hear in this group
    confidential, sharing it with no one unless doing so
    is a matter (literally) of life and death.
We will use what we learn in this group to contribute
    even more fully to the overall ministry of

_____

    (Put your congregation's name here.)
We will respect one another's schedules by
    beginning and ending on time.

Contents

How to Use this Course	7
1. Knowing God—The Master Architect	17
2. Knowing God—By Name	24
3. Knowing God—His Love Letter to Us	31
4. Knowing God—The Final Word	38
Helps for the Leader	45
Session 1	47
Session 2	50
Session 3	53
Session 4	58

How to Use This Course

Three ingredients will make it possible for you to maximize the usefulness of this course.

❖ 1—Prayer

Only as God invades our lives and touches our hearts can we grow up in Him. Ask and keep on asking for the Holy Spirit's direction and help as you approach His Word. Even if you work through the questions in this study on your own (and perhaps especially then), you must rely on God to do His work in you, His holy work of drawing you to Himself. He's the only one who can connect us to Himself and keep that connection strong. He's the only one who can connect us to our brothers and sisters in the faith and keep those connections strong. We need to ask Him to do that.

❖ 2—Care

That is, care for one another in your group. Dietrich Bonhoeffer once wrote, "Christianity means community through Jesus Christ and in Jesus Christ . . . we belong to one another only through and in Jesus Christ."

Only God can create the kind of care, the kind of community, the kind of connectedness that we see modeled by the early Christian church. It's His gift to His people. We can't make it happen, no matter how slick our techniques, no matter how smooth our approach.

But we can, by God's grace, encourage the kind of atmosphere, the kind of love and acceptance, in which His people come to know one another as brothers and sisters in the faith and not as third or fourth cousins.

❖ 3—As We Share

How does that kind of love happen? We cannot drum it up by our own effort, no matter how up-to-date our methodology. Neither can we force any believer or group of believers to talk about their faith with one another, to share their needs and hurts with each other, or to admonish and console one another. We can, however, use what we know about human relationships to create a safe haven, an island of time and place, in which God's people can relax, get to know one another, and, eventually, feel free to let down their guard.

In this kind of setting, participants can experience the freedom to talk about their hurts and their faith with each other, if they choose to do that. They can encourage one another in the one true faith, just as the early Christians did and as the holy apostles also urge us to do as God's chosen people today (1 Thessalonians 4:18; 5:11).

❖ On to the Practical

As you develop small group ministry in your congregation, you need to keep an overarching vision in mind. But to get small group Bible study off the ground, and to keep it functioning effectively, you also need to think through some practical considerations.

Leadership

Talk with your pastor about this. He has both the right and the duty to oversee any Bible study program in your congregation. He himself may lead some groups. And he may decide to delegate some leadership tasks, approving those who will teach and taking care to see that they receive adequate training.

In general, all those who lead small group Bible studies will be people who
- demonstrate an understanding of Law and Gospel, sin and grace, not just intellectually, but in the relationships with God and with other people ;
- demonstrate an ability to communicate the truths of the Scriptures clearly;
- express a desire to be used by God to disciple others;
- show a commitment to the entire congregation and submission to the authority of the pastor, not competing with other leaders or programs;
- know or be willing to learn techniques that enable adults to examine and apply their faith to their daily lives;
- pray for the group and the congregation regularly;
- have time to plan, prepare, and lead a small-group Bible study on an ongoing, consistent basis;
- demonstrate the emotional and spiritual maturity to accept responsibilities of leadership, to receive direction and sometimes criticism with wisdom and grace, to share personal strengths and weaknesses with appropriate vulnerability, and to respond to others with Christ-like humility and love.

Setting

Many people find a home conducive to the relaxed, casual atmosphere you want to foster. In any case, you will need a meeting place where
- from 6–10 people can sit comfortably and see one another as they converse;
- the chairs are comfortable;
- the room is suitably lighted, ventilated, and at a comfortable temperature;
- coffee, tea, or soft drinks and an occasional snack can be served without danger of damaging carpets or upholstery;

- children can be adequately supervised while they play away from the Bible study group.

Supplies

Everyone who attends should bring his or her own Bible. In addition you will need
- copies of this Study Guide for everyone (note the leader's materials in the back of this guide);
- pens or pencils, one for everyone;
- songbooks, hymnals, and perhaps an instrument to accompany singing during worship times;
- an empty chair or two placed prominently to remind everyone of the opportunity to invite guests—in particular, unchurched friends or relatives.

❖ That First Meeting

The first time you're together, you will want to spend some time getting to know one another and establishing rules for the group.
- Introduce yourselves to one another. Do this even if only one person is unfamiliar to the others. Tell your name. Tell a little about your family. And tell how you've come to be in the group. Use a timer and allow each person to speak for about one minute.
- Agree on ground rules about questions like these:
  Is it okay to smoke?
  Who will bring snacks? How often?
  Will we provide childcare? If so, how? Will we take turns, hire someone and agree to all chip in to pay for it? Or?
  Will we meet in one location? Take turns hosting the group? Or?
  When will we begin? End? (Include dates and also times.)
- Read the "By Mutual Agreement" statement located on page 3 of this guide. Talk it over until everyone under

stands it and you truly have reached mutual agreement Promise to reread this agreement as you begin each session, at least the first several times you get together.
- Talk about participation. This study asks group members to work with partners or with three or four other people. Agree to listen to one another with respect. Also agree to allow one another the freedom to "pass" on any question for any reason without having to state that reason.
- Remind one another that everyone is entitled to an opinion. However, in this group all human opinions must take a back seat to the Holy Scriptures. You will share lots of thoughts and feelings with one another during the next few weeks. At least you will, if this course is written well, and your leader(s) encourage participation as they should. Even so, we believe that absolute truth exists and that it can be known because the God who created the universe has revealed the truth for us in His Word. We bow to His wisdom. We submit to His truth.

❖ Elements of Small-Group Bible Studies

Most groups spend 60–90 minutes together in these four activities:
- Worship
- Bible study
- Prayer
- Fellowship

Worship (5–15 minutes)

As most small-group Bible studies begin, participants spend a few minutes in worship. Often this includes singing, especially if someone in the group can play the guitar or piano. If the group does not include a musician, someone the group can usually find an alternative that will allow everyone to join in singing two or three hymns or songs. Some groups find that they manage to sing quite well a cappella. Some use prerecorded accompaniment tracks from cassette tapes or CDs.

Keep in mind, though, that worship involves much more than simply singing a few random songs. Worship should help participants quiet their hearts as the Lord prepares them to hear what He will say to them in His Word.

Therefore, opening worship will almost always include a prayer for His peace and for hearts ready to receive His truth.

Bible Study (40–60 minutes)

Our relationship with our Lord deepens as we immerse ourselves in His Word. In that Word He confronts us with our sin and then comforts us with His forgiving love in our Savior. Small-group Bible study at its best provides for both those processes to take place.

Materials appropriate for small-group study avoid lecture. Rather, they involve a mix of individual thought and writing, one-on-one discussions, and give-and-take conversations by the whole group. The leader facilitates, asks questions, provides nuggets of insight to push the group's process forward, and prays for participants while they think and talk with one another.

Prayer—(5–10 minutes)

In the small-group Bible study process, God's Word touches the hearts of His people. It probes pockets of hurt and sometimes of hardness. God's people talk with one another about life's most important issues. We think and laugh together. We question and cry together. It's only natural that we pray together too. It's not only natural, but necessary.

This kind of prayer models itself after that of the early church:

> They raised their voices together in prayer to God. . . . After they prayed, the place where they were meeting was shaken. And they were all filled with the Holy Spirit and spoke the word of God boldly. (Acts 4:24, 31)

Committed by God's grace, to one another, and to the truth of His Word, God's people asked their Lord to intervene in their lives. Together they asked for His specific help with specific challenges and needs. They united their hearts in praise to Him for all He had done and for all that He had promised yet to do. They received from Him the power they needed to live as His witnesses in a world that is, even now for the most part, hostile to the claims Christ. We join them in the same kind of prayer.

Fellowship (10–20 minutes)

Christian fellowship means so much more than this spring's softball league or last Friday's fish fry. Of course, there is nothing wrong with playing softball or sharing a meal with other believers. But God intends that Christian fellowship (*koinonia*) cut more deeply below life's surface than that.

As we said earlier, only God can create genuine fellowship. It's His gift to His people. We can, however, provide unstructured time over coffee or lemonade before and after the more formal group time. This will free participants to laugh together, to cry together, to ask one another about ongoing personal and family concerns and simply to enjoy one another as members of God's family.

We witness spontaneously to one another about what God has done for us in Christ's cross and, then too, about what He is doing for us in our day-to-day lives. We have the chance to share specific prayer requests one-on-one and to become aware of needs God would use us to meet for each other. In short, we have a chance to be the church, the family of God, for one another.

❖ As You Begin This Course

What does it mean to know God?
Can I really know Him?
Does He want me to know Him?
What difference will it make if I do know Him?
How can I know God—not just know *about* Him, but *know Him*?

All kinds of people down through history have asked questions like these. Some have had their questions answered. Some have died, still not sure of the answers.

This course will guide you through a four-session quest for answers. As you move along, you will follow a path charted by God Himself. He will reveal Himself to you. You see, He wants you to know Him. He truly does!

In session 1, we will look at what nature tells us about God. Just as one might deduce quite a lot about an architect by studying the architect's buildings, we can learn quite a lot about God by studying what He has made.

In session 2, we will look in-depth at another set of clues about God—His names. The name Frank Lloyd Wright says something to those who know architecture. In a much, much fuller sense, God has revealed Himself by sharing His name with His people.

That revelation brings with it a unique picture of God—who He is and what He is like. It evokes trust. As one who knew Him well once wrote, "Those who know Your name will trust in You" (Psalm 9:10).

In session 3 we will look at what God has told us about Himself in the written record He has given us, the Holy Scriptures. One could learn a great deal about Frank Lloyd Wright by reading essays and articles he has written and by listening to interviews he gave. We, too, can learn much about God by reading the written revelation He has given us.

In session 4 we will cut to the very heart of who God is as we see what He has shown us about Himself in Jesus Christ, our Savior. Most architecture buffs would love a chance to meet their favorite architect in person. Christians believe that God has come to us in the flesh. He has come to us in person, in Jesus. Not only that, He has adopted us into His very own family and has written our names into His will. He has made us His heirs in Christ.

When all is said and done, we can know God only in Jesus. That's why Jesus came to us. We could not come to Him. We could not know Him. And we didn't even want to. But He has come to us. May God reveal Himself to you as you work through this course with other believers. May you know God better and better and trust Him more and more as a result of the time you spend together in His Word.

> Now this is eternal life: that they may know You, the only true God, and Jesus Christ, whom you have sent. (John 17:3)

Knowing God— The Master Architect 1

Setting Our Sights

In this session we will explore the difference between knowing *about* God and *knowing Him*. We will review the part that nature and our conscience play in our knowledge of God. We will ask ourselves why we want to know God better and then look at some ways that might happen in our individual lives.

Getting Started

Find a partner. If possible, choose someone other than a close family member. If you do not know one another, introduce yourselves. Then, just to break the ice, take turns completing this sentence: *The most unusual building I ever saw or visited was . . .*

Digging In

Just as one might learn a lot about an architect or master builder by studying that person's buildings, we can learn a lot about God by looking at what He has made.

1. Tell your partner about a time you found yourself overawed by something in nature.

2. Tell your partner about a time you found yourself frightened by something in nature.

3. Suppose all the clues you had about God came from nature.

a. What would you conclude about the architect who designed the natural world?

b. To what feelings or actions would your conclusions lead?

____ worship   ____ service   ____ sacrifice

____ indifference ____ anger   ____ awe

____ fear, terror ____ thankfulness

_____(other)

4. Anthropologists tell us that most cultural groups worship gods of some kind or another. Mountains of gold and oceans of silver have been smelted, hammered, formed, and shaped to represent deities supposedly worthy of worship. Parents have sometimes drowned their infants to appease a river god. High priests have thrown teenage girls into the gaping jaws of volcanoes to appease angry gods who had withheld a good harvest.

While some would try to deny God's existence, few people live without a religion of some kind. David once wrote, **The fool says in his heart, "There is no God"(Psalm 14:1)**.

a. How would you explain the fact that belief in a god or in the gods has been so common in human history?

b. Most people who know their god(s) only by what they see in nature, live and worship in fear. What part might conscience play in this fear? (See Romans 1:20–23.)

> For since the creation of the world God's invisible qualities—His eternal power and divine nature—have been clearly seen, being understood from what has been made, so that men are without excuse.
> For although they knew God, they neither glorified Him as God nor gave thanks to Him, but their thinking became futile and their foolish hearts were darkened.
> Although they claimed to be wise, they became fools and exchanged the glory of the immortal God for images made to look like—mortal man and birds and animals and reptiles. (Romans 1:20–23)

c. Reread the passage from Romans with a pencil in hand. Underline the words that bring to mind feelings like alienation, fear, anger, or rebellion. Have you ever experienced feelings like these vis-à-vis God? If you feel comfortable, share that experience with your partner.

Hitting Home

Alienated from God. That's how human beings have lived since Adam and Eve fell into sin. It's the way most people still live. We've built walls to shut our Creator out. It's lonely behind our walls. It's frightening, too.

Even though we've erected the walls, we cannot tear them down. We can't even come out from behind them. We've created our own prison.

God didn't wait for us to come to Him. He has come to us. He's broken through our walls. He's come crashing into our alienation to scatter our loneliness. God has a human face—the face of Christ.

To know God is to know Christ. To know Christ is to know God. As Jesus Himself once said, "Anyone who has seen Me has seen the Father" (John 14:9).

1. But what does it mean to know God? Let's think about that concept in terms of our human relationships first. In the blanks before each statement, write the name of someone you "know" in the sense described.

_____a. To put face and name together.

_____b. To have some facts about personal likes and dislikes.

_____c. To anticipate what the person will say or do before they say or do it, even if you've never seen them in that exact situation before.

_____d. To experience the emotions that person experiences, to grieve when they grieve, to rejoice when they succeed, to yearn as they yearn, to be moved by the things that touch them most deeply.

2. Keeping those four categories in mind, think about your relationship with God. Circle the appropriate letter below. Then as you feel comfortable in doing so, talk with your partner about why you responded as you did.

a. God knows me at this level   a   b   c   d

b. I know God at this level   a   b   c   d

3. On your own, complete these two sentences (in writing, if you can do so comfortably).

I want to know God better because . . .

The thing(s) most responsible for keeping this from happening is (are) . . .

4. How has God begun and deepened your knowledge of Him in Christ to this point in your life? What clues does this give you about how He might continue to do that? Talk about these two important questions with your partner.

> And now just as you trusted Christ to save you, trust Him, too, for each day's problems; live in vital union with Him.
>
> Let your roots grow down into Him and draw up nourishment from Him. See that you go on growing in the Lord, and become strong and vigorous in the truth you were taught. Let your lives overflow with joy and thanksgiving for all He has done. (Colossians 2:6–7 TLB)

Wrapping Up

Dear Lord,

You know me so much better than I know myself. Thank You that in Jesus You've shown me what You're really like. As I think about knowing You, Lord, I'd like

Please keep me from

Help me to

All this by Your grace, Lord Jesus, not in my own effort. Amen.

The Extra Mile

Read and think about some or all of the passages below. They all talk about knowing God. What is the Holy Spirit speaking to your heart through each?

Matthew 11:25–30
Luke 10:21–24
1 John 4:6–21

Knowing God— By Name

❖ Setting Our Sights

In this session we will explore the importance of knowing God as He has revealed Himself to us in His names. We will think through the truth the psalmist expressed as he wrote, "Those who know Your name [Lord] will trust in You" (Psalm 9:10). And we will look at ways that might happen more and more fully in our individual lives.

Getting Started

Think of someone you know well.

1. Take two minutes. In the space below, write down everything you can about that person.

2. Review your list. Identify how you first learned what you know. These codes may help you:

P — The person told you him/herself.
A — Another person told you.
I — Intuition; you guessed it and your guess proved right.
ES — Experiences you and your friend shared together revealed this.
O — You learned this in some other way.

3. Review your list and circle every item you have marked **ES**. How important are shared experiences as we get to know others? Discuss this with a partner—perhaps the person with whom you spoke the last time your group got together.

Digging In

God has always wanted His people to know about Him. Even more, though, He has wanted us to know *Him*. From the beginning of history, long before most of His people had access to the written Scriptures, God revealed Himself by sharing His names with His people. By thinking about those names, God's people learned to know Him.

More often than not, God tied a particular name to an experience He shared with His people. In this way, the name took on even greater significance, meaning, power.

Choose one of the names from the chart on pages 26–28. Read the Scripture text tied to it. Then think through and discuss the questions that follow.

God Almighty or God, the Mountain One
(Genesis 17:1–8)

1. What factors make God's promise to Abraham almost laughable?

2. If you had stood in Abraham's sandals, how would you have reacted to God's promise?

3. Sit with Abraham in your mind's eye under the stars. How might God's newly revealed name have helped you know and trust Him?

The Lord Your Healer
(Exodus 15:22–26)

1. Stand in the sandals of these people. What fears would have gripped your heart? (How long have you ever gone without water?)

2. God performs a miracle of mercy. Then He tacks on an additional promise—the new name He reveals to His people. Suppose your family had included young children or aging parents. Or suppose you had health concerns of your own. Remember you're out in the desert, away from civilization. What would this name have meant to your heart? Explain.

3. How might God's newly revealed name have helped you know and trust Him?

The Lord Your Shepherd
(1 Samuel 17:32–37 and Psalm 23)

1. Sit with David in your mind's eye on the hillside watching your sheep. See yourself as a teenager. What difficulties do you expect you might encounter?

2. Imagine yourself as young David, face-to-face with a wild animal that has already bloodied one or more of your sheep. How might the Lord's care for you strengthen and comfort you?

3. How might experiencing the Lord as your Shepherd in these little frays give you confidence as life's giant problems loom on the horizon?

Hitting Home

Throughout history, God has helped His people know Him by revealing His name to them.

1. Take two minutes. Write down all the names/titles for God you know.

2. Go back over your list. Circle the three names/titles you find most meaningful.

3. Take three minutes. Sit back in your chair. Relax. Close your eyes if you like. Meditate on one of the names you just circled. Recall an experience from your own life in which God "lived up to His name." Relive that experience in your mind's eye.

4. Now talk about that experience with your partner. Explain something of the trouble, the temptation, and the worry you faced. How did God live through the experience with you? What did that shared experience help you realize about your Lord?

Wrapping Up

David once told God, "Those who know Your name will trust in You, for You, LORD, have never forsaken those who seek You" (Psalm 9:10).

1. Based on the study you have just completed, what does it mean to *know God's name?* In what sense is *knowing His name* the same as *knowing Him?*

2. Which name of God would you like to know (in the fullest sense) better? How could that happen?

The Extra Mile

Read and think about some or all of the passages below. All talk about God's name. What is the Holy Spirit speaking to your heart through each?

Numbers 6:23–27
Psalm 20
Psalm 113
Proverbs 18:10
Isaiah 9:6–7

Knowing God— His Love Letter to Us

Setting Our Sights

In this session, we will review the truth that God reveals Himself in His Word. The Holy Scriptures are God's love letter, a love letter written to each of us, personally. As we read it in that way, the Holy Spirit deepens our relationship with Him.

Getting Started

Find a partner. If possible, choose someone other than a close family member. To break the ice, take turns telling one another about an experience in which someone sent you a note expressing friendship, care, or love. Was the message expected or unexpected? How did it affect you? How did it affect your relationship with the person who sent it.

Take a moment to jot a few notes to yourself here. Then share your thoughts with a partner.

Digging In

God wants us to know Him, to know Him intimately and personally. His creation and our consciences tell us about Him, but in a blurred and indistinct way. Down through history God has shared His names with His people. Those names give us a clearer picture of our God. They help us to know Him.

In the Holy Scriptures our Lord discloses Himself much more fully. He tells us what He's like. He shares with us what He thinks. He shows us some of what He's been up to throughout history.

In one sense, the Bible is like an autobiography. In another sense, it is like a love letter, God's love letter. And it's addressed to you. Personally.

Let's think about those two views of Holy Scripture for a few moments. Fill in the blank spaces in the chart on the next page on your own. Then take a little time to talk with your partner about what you have written.

Hitting Home

1. Review the chart you just completed.

a. From what you know of the Scriptures, would you consider them more like an autobiography or a love letter? Explain.

b. What elements of each do you see in Scripture?

	Autobiography	Love Letter
1 What might motivate you to write this?	To share my experiences; To let others know about my personality and character; To share my story with future generations; To . . .	Thoughts and feelings About the person to whom I'm writing; Promises to the one I love; Hopes for our future together; Feelings of affection and admiration . . .
2 What might you include?		
3 What elements would be somewhat the same? Why?	Both probably talk about important events and people in the writer's life; Both open up windows that let us see into the writer's mind and heart; both . . .	
4 In what ways would they differ? Why?		

❖❖❖❖❖❖❖❖❖❖❖❖❖❖❖❖❖❖❖❖❖❖❖❖❖❖❖

> O my people, hear my teaching; listen to the words of my mouth. I will open my mouth in parables, I will utter hidden things, things from of old—what we have heard and known, what our fathers have told us.
>
> We will not hide them from their children; we will tell the next generation the praiseworthy deeds of the LORD, His power, and the wonders He has done. . . .
>
> which He commanded our forefathers to teach their children, so the next generation would know them, even the children yet to be born, and they in turn would tell their children.
>
> Then they would put their trust in God and would not forget His deeds but would keep His commands. They would not be like their forefathers—a stubborn and rebellious generation, whose hearts were not loyal to God, whose spirits were not faithful to Him. (Psalm 78:1–8)

❖❖❖❖❖❖❖❖❖❖❖❖❖❖❖❖❖❖❖❖❖❖❖❖❖❖❖

2. Listen while someone in your group reads Psalm 78:1–8 aloud.

a. Now review these verses on your own. Underline the words and phrases that describe the kind of relationship with Him God works in our hearts through His Word. (You should find at least four.)

b. Did the words you underlined describe mostly knowledge, attitudes, or actions?

c. What kind of "knowing" do you suppose the psalmist had in mind as he wrote, "so the next generation would know them"?

d. How is that kind of knowing connected to attitudes and actions?

e. What "praiseworthy deeds of the LORD" would you most like to share with the next generation? Explain.

3. Someone has said that God gave us His Book to confront the comfortable and to comfort the distressed. God's Word to us is both a word of Law and a word of Gospel.

a. When might someone write a love letter that confronts in no uncertain terms the one who receives it?

b. If you feel comfortable in doing so, tell about a time God's Law did that for you. Focus on how your relationship with God grew during the experience, uncomfortable though that experience may have been.

35

c. What kind of comfort can a love letter provide? In what kinds of circumstances might one reread and reread such a letter?

d. Tell about a time God's Word comforted you. Focus primarily on how your relationship with God deepened during that experience.

Wrapping Up

Take a few minutes to read **Psalm 121**. Think of the words as God's love letter to you. As you read, think about how you would complete this sentence:

***This psalm helps me know God in a deeper way because in it God assures me* . . .**
Jot your thoughts below. Then talk with your partner about what you've written.

> I lift up my eyes to the hills—
>   where does my help come from?
> My help comes from the LORD,
>   the Maker of heaven and earth.
> He will not let your foot slip—
>   He who watches over you will not slumber;
> indeed, He who watches over Israel
>   will neither slumber nor sleep.
> The LORD watches over you—
>   the LORD is your shade at your right hand;
> the sun will not harm you by day,
>   nor the moon by night.
> The LORD will keep you from all harm—
>   He will watch over your life;
> the LORD will watch over your coming and going
>   both now and forevermore.
>
> (Psalm 121)

The Extra Mile

In the coming days, read and think about some or all of the passages below. All talk about God's Word. What is the Holy Spirit saying to you through each?

Psalm 119:105–112
Isaiah 55:6–13
John 1:1–12
Hebrews 1:1–3

4 Knowing God—The Final Word

❖ Setting Our Sights

In this session we will focus on knowing God through His Son, Jesus Christ. We will see Jesus as the Father's last and most important Word to us. We will explore ways to know God better as we come into a deeper and deeper relationship with Jesus—all by His grace.

Getting Started

Take a moment for a "What If . . . " exercise. Sit back. Close your eyes, if you feel comfortable doing so. Imagine that as you begin your time together God Himself suddenly came into your group visibly and in all His glory. In your mind's eye, picture Him as He appears on the scene, a hundred or so of the holy angels with Him.

As you imagine this, think of how you might react. What thoughts, feelings, joys, and fears might rise in your heart? What actions might you take? In the space below, jot down some of the things you might think, say, or do.

Digging In

1. The prophet Isaiah stood unexpectedly in the Lord's presence one day. Read about that experience from **Isaiah 6:1–8**.

   a. If Isaiah could have chosen three words to describe his reaction to his experience, what words might he have chosen?

   b. Compare Isaiah's response to the response you think you would have if you found yourself suddenly whisked into the Lord's presence. How would your reaction be similar to Isaiah's? How might it differ?

2. Fear. Despair. Anxiety. Guilt. Any or all of these feelings probably spring to life in the heart of any human being who contemplates an audience in heaven's throne room.

   a. Why do you think that is?

   b. How might feelings like these get in God's way as He works at deepening our knowledge of Him, our relationship with Him?

c. How did God resolve this problem for Isaiah?

d. How has God resolved this problem for you?

Hitting Home

Human consciences shout so loudly at times that they drown out what God has told us again and again about His forgiveness and His love. Because our rebellion and fear kept us from coming to God, God came to us. Determined to have the last word, determined to speak a language our hardened hearts could understand, our Lord invaded human history.

Read about that from **Hebrews 1:1–3**.

> In the past God spoke to our forefathers through the prophets at many times and in various ways, but in these last days He has spoken to us by His Son, whom He appointed heir of all things, and through whom He made the universe.
>
> The Son is the radiance of God's glory and the exact representation of His being, sustaining all things by His powerful Word. After He had provided purification for sins, He sat down at the right hand of the Majesty in heaven. (Hebrews 1:1–3)

1. Boil these words down to their essence. Which summary statement below comes closest to the way you might summarize the meaning of the first few verses of Hebrews?

_____ a. Jesus created and sustains the world.
_____ b. God spoke through the Old Testament prophets.
_____ c. God has appointed Jesus to rule the universe.
_____ d. God wants us to know Him through His Son, Jesus, our Savior.
_____ e. _____

2. The New Testament fairly bursts with this truth. The Holy Spirit says, "You want to know God, to really know Him? Then look to Jesus. He's the exact answer to all your questions about God. He's God Himself—God with a human face."

To know Jesus is to know God. We know Jesus in what He has said and in what He has done. Take a few minutes right now to think that through. Fill in both boxes (below/on p. 42) with as many different answers as you can.

What Jesus Did

❖❖❖❖❖❖❖❖❖❖❖❖❖❖❖❖❖❖❖❖❖❖❖❖❖❖❖
What Jesus Said

❖❖❖❖❖❖❖❖❖❖❖❖❖❖❖❖❖❖❖❖❖❖❖❖❖❖❖

3. Now look back over the lists you just made. Complete these four sentences in four different ways, based on what you've seen in Jesus through your study of the Scriptures.

I know God is _____ because

I know God thinks _____ because

I know God feels _____ because

I know God does _____ because

4. Choose one or two of the sentences you just completed. Read what you've written to

your partner and explain why you find that truth especially meaningful in your life from day to day.

Wrapping Up

❖❖❖❖❖❖❖❖❖❖❖❖❖❖❖❖❖❖❖❖❖❖❖❖❖

Therefore, there is now no condemnation for those who are in Christ Jesus. (Romans 8:1)

❖❖❖❖❖❖❖❖❖❖❖❖❖❖❖❖❖❖❖❖❖❖❖❖❖

As you conclude, return to the "What If . . ." exercise with which you began. Follow these steps:

1. Read **Romans 8:1** to yourself. Underline the words *now* and *no*.

2. Reread the verse aloud with your partner. Emphasize the words you underlined.

3. Underline the words *in Christ Jesus*.

4. Reread the verse aloud with everyone in your group. Emphasize all the underlined words.

5. Now sit back, take a deep breath, and think about finding yourself suddenly in God's visible presence. Picture yourself kneeling before His throne.

a. What difference does knowing Jesus make as you worship there?

b. What difference does knowing Jesus make as you leave His throne room to go back to your everyday activities, problems, and relationships?

The Extra Mile

In the coming days, read and think about some or all of the passages below. All talk about the Lord Jesus. All will help you know Him better. What is the Holy Spirit saying to you through each?

John 10:11–18
John 14:1–4
John 15:1–11
John 17:20–26
Philippians 2:5–11

Helps for the Leader

1—The Master Architect

❖ Getting Started

(*About 4 minutes.*) Read the session goal statement to the group ("Setting Our Sights"). Explain that this statement outlines the session in broad strokes. When everyone in a group knows where they plan to go together, they're more likely to get there.

Help participants find a partner. Encourage them to chose someone other than a close family member. If some in the group may not know one another, allow everyone time to introduce themselves to their partner. Then ask each partner-pair to complete the ice breaker sentence printed in their guide:

The most unusual building I ever saw or visited was . . .

❖ Digging In

Read the opening paragraph to the group. Then lead the partner-pairs through the set of questions printed in the Study Guide. Allot time carefully and insofar as is possible, keep the discussion moving along.

1. (*One minute each.*) Tell your partner about a time you found yourself overawed by something in nature.

2. (*One minute each.*) Tell your partner about a time you found yourself frightened by something in nature.

3. (*About 3 minutes.*) Work together as a group on these two questions. If possible, write the group's answers to *a* on a large sheet of poster paper.

b. (*About 3 minutes.*) Let individuals respond by checking

and/or writing responses in their Study Guides. Then invite volunteers to share ideas with the entire group.

4. Read the opening paragraphs to the group.

a. (*2 minutes.*) Let participants speculate.

b. (*2 minutes.*) Call attention to the Romans passage in the Study Guide. Let participants share thoughts with their partners.

c. (*5 minutes.*) Allow time for participants to underline the passage from Romans as the Study Guide suggests. Ask volunteers to share with the whole group the words and phrases they marked.

Encourage participants to share with their partners thoughts about their own experiences of alienation from God.

❖ Hitting Home

Have a volunteer read the first four paragraphs in this section.

1. (*2 minutes.*) Give participants time to work through this exercise on their own first. It may help if you give examples from your own relationships as you explain the activity. Everyone in the room probably *knows* the president or the prime minister—we can connect the face with the name. Perhaps you *know* your next-door neighbor well enough to bake his favorite cake and present it to him on his birthday without being reminded. You may *know* your supervisor or a long-time co-worker well enough to guess what she might say or do in the face of an unexpected difficulty or bonus. You probably *know* your best friend, your sister, or your spouse even more deeply—to the point of feeling what they feel, wanting what they want.

2. (*4 minutes.*) Read the directions to the group. Then give individuals time to respond. After everyone has had time to think, invite partners to talk about their responses with one another.

3. (*5 minutes.*) Allow time for individuals to complete the sentences in writing.

4. (*4 minutes.*) Point out the critical nature of these questions. Suggest participants refer to the passage from Colossians 2 as they think through this issue.

To summarize and wrap up after participants have wrestled with these questions, call attention to the opening phrase of the Colossians passage: **Just as you received Christ Jesus as Lord, continue to live in Him** . . .

Remind the group of how they received Christ Jesus—by grace. Jesus came to us; we did not come to Him. Now we continue to live in Him by that same grace. We come to know Him—personally and intimately. And we come to be like Him, too, all by the same precious grace of God, especially as He works in our hearts through His Word. As we read that Word, we intentionally focus on getting to know our Savior better and better. That's how we sink our roots more and more deeply into the soil of God's love and receive from Him the power to grow up in Christ-likeness.

❖ Wrapping Up

(*5 minutes.*) Give individuals time to complete the prayer by filling in the blanks in the Study Guide. Encourage participants to pause and pray their prayer when they have finished it. If some partner-pairs wish to pray with one another, let them do so. You might offer this as an option.

❖ The Extra Mile

Before participants leave, spend some time in group prayer as well. Read the suggestions that appear in the introduction of this guide.

The passages referenced in this section could form the foundation for the participants' devotional reading during the coming week. Suggest that as a possibility. Also suggest that as they read any part of Scripture, they look for what God is telling us about Himself.

2—His Name

❖ Getting Started

(*About 7 minutes.*) Read aloud the goal statement for the lesson ("Setting Our Sights"). Then move directly into the opening activity.

1. Ask participants to choose someone they know well (e.g., a spouse, sibling, or best friend) as they begin the activity. After two minutes, call time. Ask that the group move to the next part of this introductory activity.

2. Encourage the group to use the symbols given here and to add some of their own if they find it appropriate. Allow group members a minute or two to complete the activity.

3. Have everyone select a partner for this activity. Give participants the option of choosing the person they worked with in session 1 or of choosing new partners. After allowing two or three minutes for them to talk together, ask for observations from the whole group.

❖ Digging In

(*About 15 minutes.*) Read the three opening paragraphs aloud to the group. Then ask everyone to turn to the chart on pages 26–28. Ask that each partner-pair read one of the three texts and together work through the three questions that follow it.

When everyone has had time to complete the assignment, ask each group for a summary of what they found and for any observations they wish to offer.

50

Stress the idea that God shared experiences with His people then just as He wants to do with us today. As He revealed His names during these experiences, His people came to know Him better and better. The better we know God, the more we can relax in His love, the more we trust Him.

❖ Hitting Home

(*15 minutes.*) Read the opening paragraph aloud.

1. Ask individuals to take two minutes to do this. When the time has passed, ask for the group's attention. Have partner-pairs share their lists, adding any new names or titles to their individual lists.

Note that technically *YHWH* is the only name for God in the Old Testament. The other words we think of as names are really titles instead.

English Bibles once added vowels to YHWH and translated the word as "Jehovah." Today, it's usually translated as "Lord" (note the small caps). Our English word *lord* is a title. Nevertheless, God intended His name, YHWH, as just that—His personal name. The Hebrew can be translated "I Am Who I Am" (see Exodus 3:13ff.) or "The One Who Makes It Happen."

Seven, eight, or more times in the Old Testament, YHWH added modifiers to His name (e.g., The Lord Your Healer; The Lord Your Banner; The Lord Your Sanctifier; The Lord Your Righteousness).

In the New Testament, of course, we find the precious name of Jesus. This combines the first part of the Hebrew word YHWH with the Hebrew word *shuah*, or "salvation". Thus the name *Jesus* might arguably be translated, "The Lord (YHWH) Saves."

2. Invite participants to do this on their own.

3. Again, invite individuals to complete this exercise. Note that one thing that gets in our way as we seek to know God better is the tendency in our culture toward busyness, toward activity, and away from thoughtfulness and medita-

tion. Encourage those who have had a hectic day to take a few deep breaths and ask God to calm their hearts and minds so they can reflect more effectively during the exercise.

4. After three minutes or so, quietly call for the group's attention. Ask that they share their experiences with a partner as the Study Guide directs.

❖ Wrapping Up

(*About 5 minutes.*) Read the verse from Psalm 9 aloud to the group.

1. Have individuals write their answers to the questions directly in their Study Guides. After about two minutes, ask for comments from volunteers. What insights have they gained?

2. Again, allow a few minutes for individual reflection and writing. Then ask for volunteers to share their thoughts.

❖ The Extra Mile

(*About 3 minutes.*) As you conclude the study, ask that the partner-pairs pray together. Encourage individuals to share general prayer needs with their partner. Also encourage them to pray specifically about their partner's answer to question 2—ways in which each partner would like to know God more fully.

When each set of partners has finished praying, you might want to lead the group in the Lord's Prayer. Ask that the group pray it a bit slower than usual, focusing especially on the petition, "Hallowed (holy) be Thy name."

Again today, point out the passages in the last section of this lesson. All focus on God's name in some way. Suggest that the readings become part of everyone's devotional life during the coming week. Also suggest that as they read any part of Scripture, they look for names or titles by which God wants to reveal more of Himself to them.

3—His Love Letter to Us

❖ Getting Started

(*About 5 minutes.*) Read aloud the goal statement for this session ("Setting our Sights"). Then give participants a few moments to find a partner. Read the ice breaker activity from the Study Guide and remind the group that the last discussion centered around the ways God reveals Himself to us in His names. As we walk through the experiences of life conscious of His presence and His desire to strengthen and help us, our relationship with Him as our Shepherd, Savior, Counselor, Father, Redeemer, and Friend grows.

Give individuals in the group one minute each to talk with a partner about a time God did that for them personally this past week. As always, note that anyone who would rather not share may simply say, "Pass." Encourage partners to respect one another's decisions to do that.

❖ Digging In

(*About 10 minutes.*) The opening paragraphs review the main points from sessions 1 and 2 and sets up the introduction to today's focus—God's revelation of Himself in His Word. Read them aloud to the group.

Then have participants turn to the chart on pp. 16–17. Ask that partners work together to complete the chart, which compares Scripture to both an autobiography and a love letter. Encourage participants to fill in the blank boxes and, as time will allow, to add to the ideas already printed in some of the boxes on the chart.

Allow about five minutes, then ask for the group's attention. Talk together about how individuals completed their charts. In most cases, the group will come to a consensus. There really are no right or wrong answers.

As you guide the discussion, stress the idea that love letters are by their very nature much more personal. Also accent the thought that a person who sends a love letter usually has one basic goal in mind—to deepen the relationship between sender and receiver.

Move from this discussion directly into the next section.

> As you lead the discussion for this session, you will find it helpful to remember that the terms *Word of God* and *Holy Scripture* are not synonymous.
>
> The Bible is, of course, just what it claims to be—the inerrant, inspired, infallible Word of God. It is our only trustworthy guide for faith and life.
>
> The Bible is the Word of God. However, the Word of God is not limited to the Bible. The Scriptures, for example, call Jesus the "Word of God." On Sunday morning your pastor proclaims the Word of God to your congregation.
>
> When human beings speak God's Word to us, we must carefully align what they say up against the Holy Scriptures to make sure the two agree. Scripture is infallible; people are not. Nevertheless, God uses His Word as that word is spoken by His human servants to strengthen our hearts.
>
> It may not be necessary to explain this distinction to your group. If, however, the discussion takes certain twists and turns, you may want to take the time needed to go over these concepts.

❖ Hitting Home

1. (*2 minutes.*) As the group talks about these questions, acknowledge that in Scripture we see elements of both. God's

purpose in giving us the Scriptures involves much more than simply sharing historical information.

The Holy Scriptures do, of course, contain many historical facts. They tell about God's activity since before the world's creation. Still, God gave us the Scriptures for another reason—to deepen His relationship with us.

2. (*10 minutes.*) Have someone read **Psalm 78:1–8** aloud. Then ask everyone to reread the psalm and think through the questions printed in the Study Guide as they underline phrases and jot down their thoughts. After about half the time has passed, ask volunteers to share their ideas with the group.

Accent the thought that "knowing" in the sense the psalmist used it involves relationship, involves intimacy. That kind of knowing shows itself in a person's attitude and actions. When we *know* God in this sense, we become more and more like Him. We share His attitudes. We do what Jesus would do if He faced our decisions and circumstances. We think and act in these ways, not because we must, but because that's who we are. It's who He's made us to be as new creatures in Christ.

The more intimately we *know* our Lord, by His grace and at His initiative, the more like Him we become.

3. (*15 minutes.*) This section touches briefly on the all-important concepts of Law and Gospel. In order to read God's Book in the way that will benefit us most powerfully, we must keep in mind the truth that those who love us sometimes confront us and sometimes comfort us. They tell us what we need to hear even when that's inconvenient or risky.

Ask participants to read through the questions printed in this section on their own and jot down a word or two to remind them of their responses. After two minutes or so, ask that they discuss their thoughts with their partners.

As always, remind participants to share only those things they can share without feeling threatened. Anyone may pass on any given question at any time.

When two minutes remain, ask that anyone who has not yet responded to *d* skip ahead to it.

As this discussion concludes, summarize the importance of reading Scripture with the Law/Gospel distinction in mind. Remind the group that the Holy Spirit Himself must teach us how to divide Law and Gospel and apply them to our own individual lives. Each time we read the Bible or listen to a sermon, we need to ask for His presence, power, and guidance.

We especially need to remember that as God confronts us with our sin, we can confess it to Him, confident that He will forgive us for Jesus' sake. As we receive His forgiveness, we also receive His power to change, to become little by little more like Jesus every day. (See 1 John 1:8–9.)

❖ Wrapping Up

(*8 minutes.*) As you introduce this activity, ask that individuals take time to read **Psalm 121** on their own and think through their ending to the sentence. Explain that then they are to share with their partner what they have discovered. Ask that they go right from this discussion into a closing prayer with their partner.

Encourage them to share individual prayer requests, but also urge them to pray that the Holy Spirit motivate and guide them to spend time with Him in His Word each day so that they may get to know Him better.

❖ The Extra Mile

Before participants leave, spend a few moments in group prayer as well.

After prayer, point out again today that the passages at the end of this session in the Study Guide could become part of each person's devotional reading during the coming week. Suggest that as they read any part of Scripture during the coming week, they look at it as God's love letter to them—to them personally. What is He telling them about Himself? about His concern for them?

4—The Final Word

❖ Getting Started

(*About 6 minutes.*) Read the session goal statement to the group ("Setting Our Sights").

Then move directly into the introductory exercise. Ask participants to follow the directions printed in the Study Guide. Results matter more than technique. If some group members find it helpful to close their eyes and others find it more helpful to begin writing immediately, that's okay. Let everyone complete the task in the way most comfortable for them.

After about three minutes for individual work, call for the group's attention. Ask everyone to find a partner and, as they feel comfortable in doing so, share the thoughts and feelings they have jotted down with that person.

❖ Digging In

(*About 15 minutes.*) Invite participants to work through the brief study of **Isaiah 6:1–8** with their partners. Answer any questions the group raises. It will probably not be necessary to go over the material in this section of the lesson with the whole group. Remind the group, as necessary, to keep moving along.

It's important to note, however, that God resolved Isaiah's problem with sin in the same way He has resolved ours—He has forgiven His people of all guilt because of the payment Christ Jesus made for sin on Calvary. Isaiah's coal sealed God's declaration of forgiveness to His prophet. It had no special, magical power of its own.

❖ Hitting Home

Have a volunteer read the introductory paragraph from the Study Guide and a second volunteer read the words of Hebrews 1:1–3.

1. (*2 minutes.*) First give participants time to work through this exercise on their own. Then ask for comments. Statement *d* perhaps best summarizes the verses from Hebrews. Note the phrases:

In the past God spoke . . . through the prophets . . . but in these last days He has spoken to us by His Son . . . . the exact representation of His being.

2. (*10 minutes.*) Read the directions to the group. Then give individuals time to fill in the two boxes. They may include accounts of Jesus' words and actions they recall from memory, or they may want to leaf through the four gospels. Ask that they refrain from writing down lengthy, direct quotations. Rather, they may include summary statements or brief quotes that serve as summaries (e.g., "I am the Good Shepherd").

After everyone has had time to write and think, invite partners to discuss their responses with one another.

3. (*5 minutes.*) Allow time for individuals to complete the sentences in writing.

4. (*2 minutes.*) Invite participants to complete the activity described in the Study Guide with a partner. Suggest that they each give their partner a minute or so to share his or her insights.

❖ Wrapping Up

(*10 minutes.*) Read the directions as they are printed in the Study Guide and let the group follow them. After the whole group reads aloud **Romans 8:1** the first time, ask that they do so again. Encourage the group to focus on our Lord's powerful promise as they read.

The last activity in this section could probably best be handled as an individual activity or by asking partner-pairs to discuss the issues raised.

❖ The Extra Mile

Before participants leave, spend some time in group prayer. If there are any, ask that requests for specific prayer needs be included in the prayer. Then ask them to recall that when God revealed Himself to Isaiah, the prophet responded in words of confession, praise, and willingness to serve the Lord. Invite individuals in the group to join in the prayer, adding their own confession, praises, and requests that the Lord use them in His service. Suggest that those who do not wish to pray aloud nevertheless speak prayers like these silently from their hearts.

Begin the prayer yourself and then allow a time of silence in which individuals may pray aloud and during which all can pray silently.

Before everyone leaves, point out that as always the passages in this section could form the foundation for devotional reading during the coming week. Suggest that as they read these or any other parts of Scripture this week, they ask their Savior to help them know Him better.

Hear His Voice in...
God's Word for Today

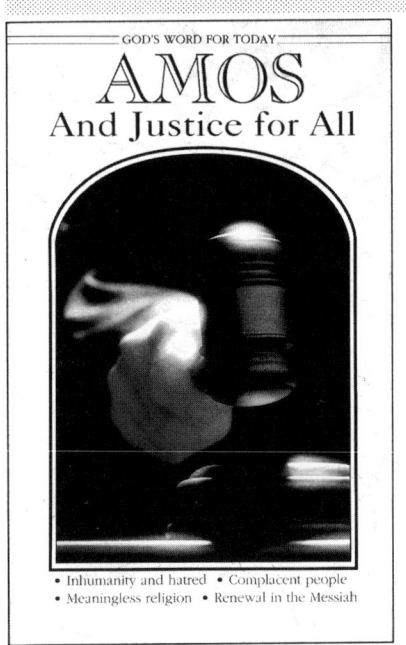

GOD'S WORD FOR TODAY
AMOS
And Justice for All

• Inhumanity and hatred • Complacent people
• Meaningless religion • Renewal in the Messiah

This series helps you hear God speaking to you today — lovingly, emphatically, personally. As you study His Word book by book, you'll find chapter-by-chapter background information; questions and learning experiences that promote exciting and challenging discussions; and activities that reveal how God speaks to the deepest concerns of your heart.

Each eight to 13 sessions

Amos: *And Justice for All*
Revelation: *Interpreting the Prophecy*
Psalms: *Conversations with God*
Genesis: *Rooted in Relationship*

Matthew: *His Kingdom Forever*
Galatians: *The Cost of Freedom*
1 Peter: *Claimed by God*
Colossians/Philemon: *Take a New Look at Christ*

CPH
3558 SOUTH JEFFERSON AVENUE
SAINT LOUIS, MISSOURI 63118-3968

© CPH 1994 H54920/1

Find Healing in . . .

THE MASTER'S Touch

Christian Support Studies for Individuals or Groups

Jesus' healing touch of love, hope and forgiveness will help you find positive solutions to the concerns weighing on your heart. As you study and share His Word, the Holy Spirit will lead you to grow in spiritual maturity and deeper faith experiences, and even reach out to those who face similar needs and concerns.

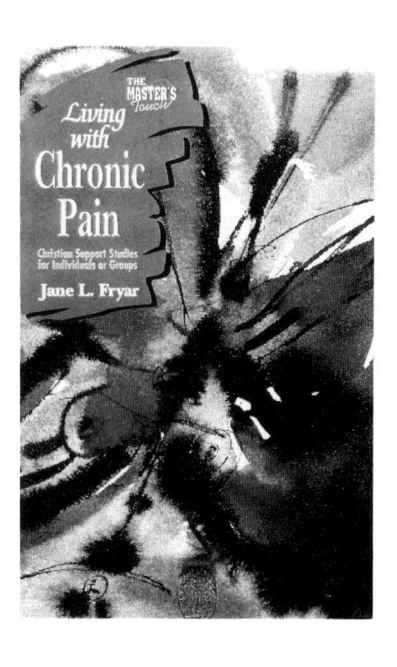

Four to five sessions each

Living with **Chronic Pain**
Suffering from **Guilt**
Living with **Change**
Coping with **Compassion Fatigue**

Living with **Compulsive Behaviors**
Discovering **Life after Divorce**
Living with **Infertility**
Surviving **Sexual Abuse**

CPH

3558 SOUTH JEFFERSON AVENUE
SAINT LOUIS, MISSOURI 63118-3968

© CPH 1994   H54920/2

FAMILY Life ISSUES

LEARN BIBLICAL PRINCIPLES TO STRENGTHEN AND SUPPORT YOUR FAMILY.

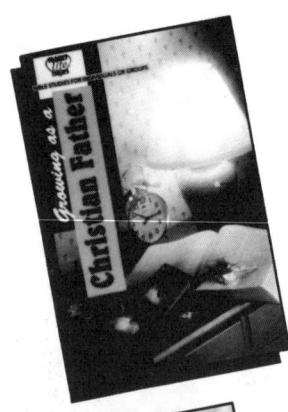

Many trends in our society today threaten the well being of the family. The new Family Life Issues series is designed to respond to these trends by giving identity, strength and direction to families through the study of God's Word.

Find encouragement for your family in this Bible study series that teaches practical skills and gives insight to build homes dedicated to Christ.

Each study contains four sessions.

Growing As a Christian Father
Overcoming Dysfunction
Growing As a Blended Family
Maximizing Media
Growing As a Christian Mother
Growing As a Single Parent
Managing Finances
Life in the Sandwich Generation

CPH
3558 SOUTH JEFFERSON AVENUE
SAINT LOUIS MISSOURI 63118-3968

H55277 © Concordia Publishing House 1994